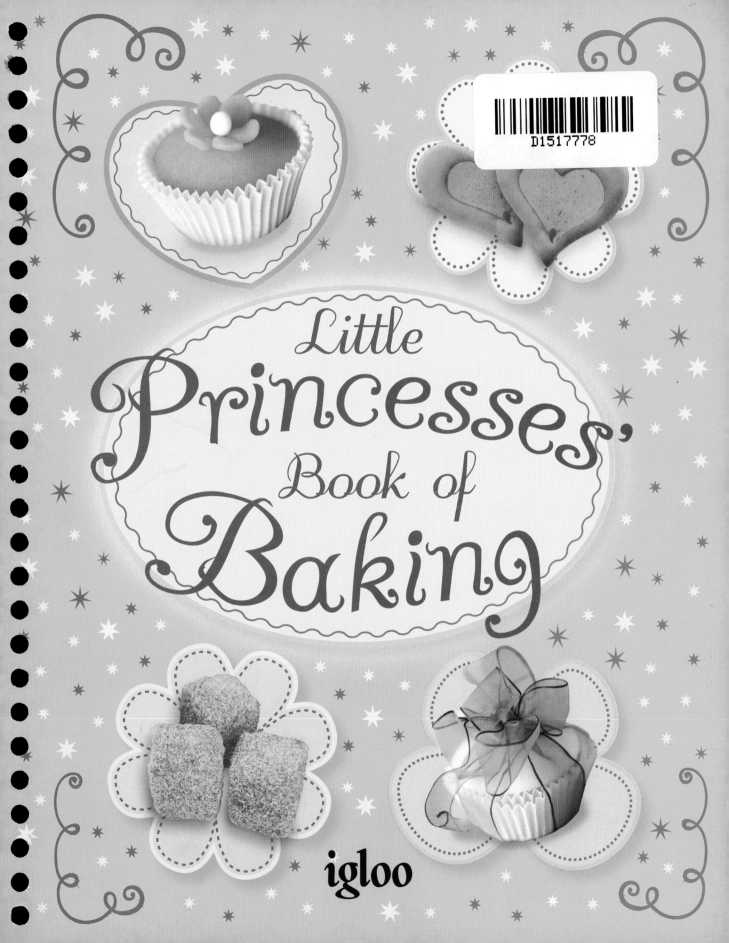

Little Princesses' Book of Baking

igloo

igloo

Published in 2012
by Igloo Books Ltd
Cottage Farm
Sywell
Northants
NN6 0BJ
www.igloo-books.com

C005 0112
10 9 8 7 6 5 4 3 2 1

ISBN: 978-0-85780-338-2

Printed and manufactured in China

Contents

Introduction   4 – 5

Snacks   6 – 31

Party Food   32 – 53

Chocolate   54 – 73

Cupcakes   74 – 95

Index   96

Introduction

Welcome to the Little Princesses Book of Baking – the most remarkably royal and fantastically fun of all cookery books!

Discover the magic of baking, with plenty of recipes fit for a Princess inside! Choose from one of four splendid sections – Snacks, Party Food, Chocolate and Cupcakes – to start. In each part of the book, you'll find recipes of every kind, from the prettiest and most perfect pink heart biscuits, to the scrummiest and gooiest macaroni bake. Enchant your taste buds with luscious loaves, the cutest of cupcakes, and even jewel-like jam biscuits, fit for the Queen of Hearts herself!

Each recipe has easy-to-follow instructions and a wonderful 'Why not try...' suggestion, to give you ideas on how to put a spellbinding twist on each tasty treat! There is a crown rating out of three on each recipe too, which shows how tricky it is to make. With practice, you'll be able to whip up every delicious delight inside in no time!

To begin, study the opposite page carefully – learn the Golden Rules, and make sure you know what each symbol means. Then, it's time to put on your apron – and your tiara – and get baking!

Golden Rules

1. Always ask an adult's permission before you start baking, or ask them to help you.
2. Wash your hands.
3. To keep your clothes clean, wear an apron.
4. Measure your ingredients carefully.
5. Always wash your hands after handling raw eggs.
6. Take extra care with scissors or knives; ask an adult to teach you or to help.
7. Always use oven gloves and be careful when using the oven.
8. When you've finished, help clean the kitchen and wash the dishes.

Symbols

Portion size

makes 8   serves 4

Preparation and cooking time

30 mins

preparation and cooking time

Difficulty

easy   medium   hard

Snacks

Golden Nuggets

difficulty

Method

Heat the oven to 200°C (180° fan) 400F, gas 6. Grease a large baking tray. Mix together the breadcrumbs, cornflakes, cheese and salt. Mix well. Put the melted butter in a bowl for dipping.

Dip the chicken pieces into the melted butter, then coat with the breadcrumb mixture until well coated. Place the chicken pieces on the baking tray in a single layer and bake for 20 minutes until crisp and golden and the chicken is cooked.

Ingredients

3 skinless, boneless chicken breasts,
cut into 3cm - 4cm / 1" - 2" pieces
100 g / 3 ½ oz / 1 cup dried breadcrumbs
30 g / 1 oz / 1 cup cornflakes, lightly crushed
50 g / 1 ¾ oz / ½ cup finely grated
Parmesan cheese
1 tsp salt
110 g / 4 oz / ½ cup butter, melted

Why not try...

adding chili flakes to the breadcrumb mixture for a spicier crunch?

Fairytale Fruit Loaf

makes
1

1 hour **10** mins
preparation and cooking time

difficulty

Method

Heat the oven to 180°C (160° fan) 350F, gas 4. Grease and line a 1 kg / 2 lb loaf tin with greaseproof baking paper. Mash the bananas and the lemon juice to a paste with a potato masher.

Beat the butter and sugar in a mixing bowl until soft and light. Whisk in the eggs and salt, until combined. Fold in the flour alternately with the banana paste. Stir in the apricots and raisins.

Spoon the mixture into the tin and bake for 50-55 minutes until cooked through. Test with a wooden cocktail stick, if it comes out clean, the cake is done. Cool in the tin for 10 minutes, then place on a wire rack to cool completely.

Ingredients

3 very ripe bananas
½ lemon, juiced
110 g / 4 oz / ½ cup butter, unsalted
75 g / 2 ½ oz / ⅓ cup caster (superfine) sugar
2 eggs, beaten
a pinch of salt
225 g / 8 oz / 2 cups self-raising flour
50 g / 1 ¾ oz / ½ cup
dried apricots, finely chopped
50 g / 1 ¾ oz / ½ cup raisins

Why not try...

using chocolate chips instead of raisins?

11

Why not try...

serving with a dollop
of sour cream?

Magical Melty Nachos

Method

For the salsa, mix together all the ingredients until well combined. Leave to stand for 10 minutes.

For the guacamole, pound the chilies, coriander, salt and onion to a fine paste in a pestle and mortar or blender. Add the lime juice to make a loose smooth mixture. Put the avocado flesh into a bowl and mash until smooth. Add the pounded mixture and stir well. Cover and chill for 10 minutes.

For the nachos, heat the oven to 220°C (200° fan) 425F, gas 7. Put the tortilla chips into a large ovenproof dish. Scatter over half of the salsa and all of the grated cheese. Cook for about 5 minutes, until the cheese has melted. Put the remaining salsa in a serving bowl. Put the guacamole in a serving bowl. Serve with the nachos and garnish with coriander.

Ingredients

For the salsa:
6 large tomatoes, deseeded and chopped
2 red chilies, deseeded and finely chopped
1 small onion, finely sliced
1 - 2 dashes Tabasco
2 cloves of garlic, finely chopped
1 large lime, juiced
1 tbsp coriander (cilantro), chopped
1 tbsp extra virgin olive oil
salt, to taste

For the guacamole and nachos:
3 mild chilies, finely chopped
1 tbsp finely chopped coriander (cilantro)
salt, to taste
1 onion, finely chopped
½ lime, juiced
3 ripe avocados
400 g / 14 oz tortilla chips
200 g / 7 oz / 2 cups Cheddar cheese, grated
coriander (cilantro) to garnish

Juicy Jewelled Slices

Method

Heat the oven to 160°C (140° fan) 325F, gas 3. Grease a deep 20 cm / 8″ square cake tin and line the base with greaseproof baking paper. Mix together the orange zest and juice and the cranberries in a small bowl.

Mix both flours with the baking powder, bicarbonate of soda and cinnamon. Separate 1 of the eggs. Put the white in a small bowl and the yolk in a mixing bowl. Add the remaining whole egg to the yolk, then add the sugar.

Whisk together until thick and foamy. Slowly pour in the oil and continue to whisk until well mixed. Gradually stir in the flour mix. Whisk the egg white until softly peaking. Fold the carrots, walnuts, cranberries (and any liquid) into the flour mixture.

Gently fold in the whisked egg white, then pour into the tin. Shake the tin to level the mixture. Bake for 1 hour until risen and firm or until a cocktail stick inserted in the middle comes out clean.

Cool in the tin for 5 minutes, then place on a wire rack, peel off the paper and leave to cool completely. Sift over a little icing sugar and cut into squares.

Ingredients

1 orange zest, finely grated
45 ml orange juice
100 g / 3 ½ oz / 1 cup cranberries
110 g / 4 oz / 1 cup wholemeal flour
110 g / 4 oz / 1 cup self-raising flour
1 tsp baking powder
1 tsp bicarbonate of (baking) soda
1 tsp ground cinnamon
2 eggs
140 g / 5 oz / ¾ cup light brown sugar
125 ml / 4 ½ fl. oz / ½ cup sunflower oil
280 g / 10 oz / 5 ½ cups carrots, finely grated
55 g / 2 oz / ½ cup walnuts, chopped
icing (confectioners') sugar

Why not try...

serving warm with
vanilla ice-cream?

The Queen's Mini Quiches

Method

Heat the oven to 200°C (180° fan) 400F, gas 6. Grease a 12 hole muffin tin. For the pastry, sift the flour into a mixing bowl and stir in the salt. Rub in the butter until the mixture resembles breadcrumbs. Add the water and mix to a dough.

Roll out the dough on a floured surface and line the tins. Prick the bases and bake for 10 minutes. Remove from the oven and allow to cool slightly.

For the filling, melt the butter in a pan and stir in the flour. Cook for 5 minutes. Gradually beat in the milk, stirring constantly until smooth. Cook for a further 5 minutes. Season to taste with salt and pepper. Beat in the cheese and basil until combined.

Spoon the filling into the pastry cases and top with a slice of tomato. Bake for 15 minutes until the filling is bubbling and the pastry is cooked.

Ingredients

For the pastry:
225 g / 8 oz / 2 cups plain (all-purpose) flour
a pinch of salt
100 g / 3 ½ oz / ½ cup butter
120-150 ml / 4 - 5 fl. oz / ½ - ⅔ cup water

For the filling:
25 g / 1 oz / ⅛ cup butter
25 g / 1 oz / ¼ cup plain (all-purpose) flour
270 ml / 10 fl. oz / 1 ⅛ cups milk
salt and pepper
55 g / 2 oz / ½ cup Cheddar cheese, grated
100 g / 3 ½ oz / ½ cup cream cheese
½ tbsp basil, chopped
3 - 4 tomatoes, sliced

Why not try...
using mozzarella cheese
and adding oregano for
a more Italian flavor?

Spectacular Savory Cakes

Method

Mix together all the ingredients, except the oil, in a mixing bowl. Form into 15-18 round patties.

Place the patties on a plate, cover with cling film and chill for 30 minutes. Heat the oil in a frying pan, about 1½cm / ½" deep and cook the patties, a few at a time, for 3-4 minutes on each side.

Serve with a chili dipping sauce and green salad.

makes

15

25 mins

preparation and cooking time

difficulty

Ingredients

1 carrot, grated
1 small onion, finely chopped
400 g / 14 oz skinless, boneless chicken breast, finely chopped
50 g / 1 ¾ oz / 1 cup fresh breadcrumbs
1 egg, beaten
198 g / 7 oz canned sweetcorn, drained
salt and pepper, to taste
oil for frying

Why not try...

using tuna instead of chopped chicken breast?

Why not try...

adding whole almonds
for a cake with more crunch?

Royal Rhubarb Loaf Cake

Method

Heat the oven to 180°C (160° fan) 375F, gas 5. Grease a 900 g / 2 lb loaf tin. Sprinkle the rhubarb with 2 tablespoons of plain flour and toss to coat the rhubarb.

Sift the remaining plain flour into a large mixing bowl with the wholemeal flour, sugar, baking powder, salt and ginger.

Melt the butter in a pan, whisk in the egg and milk and stir into the flour mixture. Fold in the ground almonds and rhubarb and pour into the tin.

Bake for 60-70 minutes. Test with a wooden cocktail stick, if it comes out clean, the cake is done. Leave in the tin for 10 minutes before turning out.

Sift over a little icing sugar just before serving.

Ingredients

350 g / 12 oz rhubarb,
cut into 2 cm / ¾" lengths
200 g / 7 oz / 2 cups plain (all-purpose) flour
75 g / 2 ½ oz / ¾ cup wholemeal flour
150 g / 5 oz / ¾ cup sugar
½ tsp baking powder
a pinch of salt
1 tbsp ground ginger
75 g / 2 ½ oz / ⅓ cup butter
1 egg
200 ml / 7 fl. oz / ⅞ cup milk
60 g / 2 oz / ½ cup ground almonds
icing (confectioners') sugar

21

Perfect Princess Pasties

makes
12

40 mins
preparation and cooking time

difficulty

Method

Heat the oven to 200°C (180° fan) 400F, gas 6. Line a large baking tray with greaseproof baking paper.

Heat the oil in a frying pan and cook the onions until starting to soften. Remove from the heat and leave to cool. Roll out the pastry on a lightly floured surface and cut out 12 circles, 10 cm / 4" in diameter.

Stir together the grated cheese and onions and season well. Divide the mixture between the pastry circles and brush the edges lightly with beaten egg. Crimp the edges together and brush with beaten egg.

Place on the baking tray and bake for about 20 minutes until the pastry is golden.

Ingredients

2 tbsp oil
225 g / 8 oz onions, chopped
500 g / 18 oz shortcrust (pie) pastry flour
225 g / 8 oz / 2 cups strong Cheddar cheese, grated
salt and pepper
1 egg, beaten

Why not try...

serving with a tangy and tasty chutney?

Ruby Rock Cakes

Method

Heat the oven to 180°C (160° fan) 350F, gas 4. Line a large baking tray with greaseproof baking paper.

Put the butter and flour into a mixing bowl and rub together with your fingertips until the mixture resembles breadcrumbs. Stir in the cranberries, orange zest, brown sugar and egg with the baking powder, cinnamon and milk. Mix together well to form a soft dough.

Divide the dough into 8 and shape each piece into a rough mound. Put onto the baking tray and bake for 15-20 minutes until pale golden. Sprinkle lightly with caster sugar while the cakes are hot.

Cool on the baking tray for a few minutes, then place on a wire rack to cool completely.

difficulty

Ingredients

100 g / 3 ½ oz / ½ cup butter, unsalted
225 g / 8 oz / 2 cups plain (all-purpose) flour
50 g / 1 ¾ oz / ½ cup dried cranberries
1 orange, finely grated zest
50 g / 1 ¾ oz / ¼ cup light brown sugar
1 large egg, beaten
1 tsp baking powder
1 tsp ground cinnamon
1 tsp milk
caster (superfine) sugar

Why not try...

using dried strawberries or raspberries?

Majestic Macaroni

Method

Heat the oven to 160°C (140° fan) 325F, gas 3. Grease a 23 cm / 9" baking tin or dish. Cook the macaroni according to the packet instructions. Drain and leave to cool slightly.

Heat the butter in a frying pan and cook the onion until soft but not browned. In a large bowl, whisk together the eggs and cream. Add the macaroni with the onion and butter remaining in the pan. Stir in the remaining ingredients until evenly mixed.

Put into the baking tin and bake for 30-40 minutes until bubbling. Remove from the oven and leave to stand for 10 minutes before cutting into squares.

Ingredients

225 g / 8 oz / 2 ¼ cups macaroni
50 g / 1 ¾ oz / ¼ cup butter
1 small onion, finely chopped
3 large eggs
400 ml / 14 fl. oz / 1 ⅔ cups cream
4 slices cooked ham,
cut into 1 ½ cm / ½" pieces
¼ tsp pepper
¼ tsp grated nutmeg
1 - 2 tsp green chili (optional), chopped
200 g / 7 oz / 2 cups Cheddar cheese, grated
50 g / 1 ¾ oz / ½ cup Parmesan cheese,
finely grated
salt and pepper, to taste

Why not try...

adding a can of chopped tomatoes for a saucier pasta bake?

makes
12

40 mins
preparation and cooking time

difficulty

The King's Cheese Crowns

Method

Heat the oven to 190°C (170° fan) 375F, gas 5. Grease a 12 hole muffin tin.

Sift the flour and baking powder into a mixing bowl. Stir in the sugar, salt, ham, peppers and three quarters of the cheese. Beat together the eggs, buttermilk and oil and pour into the dry ingredients. Stir until just combined. The mixture will be lumpy.

Spoon into the tins and sprinkle the tops with the remaining cheese. Bake for 20-25 minutes until risen and golden. Serve warm.

Ingredients

275 g / 10 oz / 2 ¼ cups plain (all-purpose) flour

1 tbsp baking powder

1 tsp sugar

½ tsp salt

110 g / 4 oz / 1 cup strong Cheddar cheese, grated

110 g / 4 oz cooked ham, chopped

90 g / 3 oz red peppers in oil, drained and chopped

2 eggs

200 ml / 7 fl. oz / ⅞ cup buttermilk

90 ml / 3 fl. oz / ⅜ cup sunflower oil

Why not try...
using chopped chorizo instead
of ham for a spicier muffin?

Why not try...

adding ground almonds to the cake mix for an extra nutty flavor?

Charming Courgette Cake

Method

Heat the oven to 180°C (160° fan) 350F, gas 4. Grease a 1 kg / 2 lb loaf tin and line the base with greaseproof baking paper.

Whisk the eggs and oil together in a mixing bowl for 5 minutes. Add the sugar and vanilla and whisk for a further 3 minutes. Fold in the flour, cinnamon, salt, courgettes and lemon zest, mixing well.

Pour the mixture into the tin. Bake for about 1 hour until risen and golden. Cool in the tin for 5 minutes, then place on a wire rack to cool completely.

For the icing, sift the icing sugar into a bowl and stir in the lemon juice to form a thin icing. Spoon the icing on top of the cake. Decorate with the almonds and leave to set.

Tips, Courgettes can hold quite a lot of water, which can affect the finished texture of the cake. If the grated courgettes seem watery, place them in a clean cloth and wring out some of the liquid into a bowl. Then add the courgettes to the cake mixture.

makes
1

1 hour
20 mins
preparation and cooking time

difficulty

Ingredients

2 eggs
120 ml / 4 fl. oz / ½ cup sunflower oil
225 g / 8 oz / 1 cup caster (superfine) sugar
½ tsp vanilla extract
350 g / 12 oz / 3 cups self-raising flour
1 tsp ground cinnamon
½ tsp salt
225 g / 8 oz courgettes (zucchini), coarsely grated
1 lemon, finely grated zest

For the icing and decoration:
150 g / 5 oz / 1 ½ cups icing (confectioners') sugar
45 - 60 ml lemon juice
25 g / 1 oz / ⅓ cup flaked (slivered) almonds, toasted

Party Food

makes

24

1 hour

preparation and cooking time

difficulty

Coconut Cubes

Method

Heat the oven to 160°C (140° fan) 325F, gas 3. Grease and line a 22 cm x 33 cm x 4 cm / 9" x 11" x 1½" baking tin with greaseproof baking paper.

Beat the sugar and butter in a mixing bowl until thick and creamy. Gradually beat in the eggs a little at a time. Stir in the milk and vanilla. Gently fold in the flour until incorporated.

Pour the mixture into the tin and smooth the top. Bake for 25-30 minutes, until golden and springy to the touch. Cool in the tin for 5 minutes, then place on a wire rack to cool completely. Trim the edges off the cake and cut into 24 squares.

For the icing, crush the raspberries in a bowl with a fork, stir in 2 tablespoons of boiling water and allow to cool for 5 minutes. Sieve the raspberry mixture into a bowl, discarding the solids.

Sift the icing sugar into a bowl. Whisk in the raspberry liquid and enough boiling water to form a smooth, thick icing. Stir in the food dye.

Spread the coconut over the base of a tray. Dip 1 cake square at a time into the icing, turning quickly to coat and allowing the excess to drip back into the bowl. Roll in coconut and place on a wire rack to set.

Ingredients

For the cake:
340 g / 12 oz / 1 ½ cups butter
265 g / 9 oz / 1 ¼ cups caster (superfine) sugar
3 eggs, beaten
135 ml / 5 fl. oz / 9 tbsp milk
1 tsp vanilla extract
340 g / 12 oz / 3 ¼ cups self-raising flour

For the icing:
125 g / 4 ½ oz / 1 cup raspberries
150 - 200 ml / 5 - 7 fl. oz / ⅔ cup boiling water
600 g / 21 oz / 6 cups icing (confectioners') sugar
few drops pink food dye

To decorate:
350 g / 12 oz / 4 cups desiccated coconut

Why not try...

adding rainbow-colored sugar sprinkles to the coconut decoration?

makes

12

35
mins

preparation and cooking time

difficulty

Sweet Honey Flapjacks

Method

Heat the oven to 180°C (160° fan) 350F, gas 4. Grease and line a shallow 20 cm / 8″ square tin with greaseproof baking paper.

Put the peanut butter, sugar, honey and oil into a pan and heat gently until melted. Stir in the remaining ingredients. Turn into the tin, level and press the mixture evenly and firmly with the back of a spoon. Bake for 25 minutes, until lightly golden around the edges.

Cool in the tin for 10 minutes, then cut into pieces while still warm. Leave to cool completely in the tin.

Ingredients

175 g / 6 oz / ⅔ cup crunchy peanut butter
75 g / 2 ½ oz / ½ cup light brown sugar
105 ml clear honey
45 ml sunflower oil
55 g / 2 oz / ½ cup dried apricots, chopped
25 g / 1 oz / ⅓ cup flaked (slivered) almonds
25 g / 1 oz / ¼ cup raisins
175 g / 6 oz / 1 ¾ cups rolled oats
75 g / 2 ½ oz / ½ cup sesame seeds

Why not try...

adding chocolate chips for a more scrumptious treat?

Why not try...

using white, milk and dark chocolate chips to decorate your wands?

Magic Wishing Wands

Method

Melt the plain chocolate in a heatproof bowl over a pan of simmering (not boiling) water. Remove from the heat.

Crumble the chocolate cake and plain cake into a bowl and stir in the melted chocolate, coconut and almonds until well combined.

Roll golf ball sized pieces of the mixture into balls. Stick a lollipop stick into each ball and chill for about 30 minutes until firm.

Sift the icing sugar into a bowl and stir in just enough water to give a thick coating consistency.

Sprinkle the sugar sprinkles onto a large plate.

Remove the balls from the fridge, dip them into the icing, then coat in the sugar sprinkles and place in a glass or cup. Leave to set.

Ingredients

100 g / 3 ½ oz plain (dark) chocolate
125 g / 4 ½ oz chocolate cake
125 g / 4 ½ oz plain cake
2 tbsp desiccated coconut
2 tbsp chopped almonds
175 g / 6 oz / 1 ¾ cups icing (confectioners') sugar
½ - 1 tbsp water
sugar sprinkles

makes

8

10 mins

preparation and cooking time

difficulty

39

Why not try...

using apricot jam, for amber-colored hearts?

Queen of Hearts Biscuits

50 mins

preparation and cooking time

difficulty

Method

Beat together the butter and sugar in a mixing bowl, then add the flour and ground almonds. Mix to a soft dough. Wrap in cling film and chill for 1 hour.

Heat the oven to 140°C (120° fan) 300F, gas 1. Line 2 large baking trays with greaseproof baking paper.

Knead the dough lightly on a lightly floured surface and divide in half. Roll out one half of the dough into a square and cut out squares with a crimped edge cutter or a sharp knife. Lightly knead the dough trimmings together and roll out again. Cut out more squares until you have about 20-24 squares. Place them on a baking tray, slightly apart.

Roll out the remaining dough and cut out the same sized squares. Using a small heart-shaped cutter, cut out the middle of each square. Place them on a baking tray.

Bake for 20-30 minutes until just golden. Cool on the baking trays for a few minutes, then place on a wire rack to cool completely. Sift a little icing sugar over the cut-out heart biscuits.

Gently warm the jam. Spread a little jam on the biscuits without the cut-out hearts. Place the top halves of the biscuits on the jam and push down gently.

Ingredients

225 g / 8 oz / 1 cup butter, unsalted
100 g / 3 ½ oz / ½ cup caster (superfine) sugar
200 g / 7 oz / 1 cup plain (all-purpose) flour
100 g / 3 ½ oz / ¾ cup ground almonds
110 g / 4 oz / ½ cup strawberry or raspberry jam (jelly)

To decorate:
icing (confectioners') sugar

Why not try...

using mango or kiwi for a more tropical taste?

Cream Castle Cake

Method

Heat the oven to 180°C (160° fan) 350F, gas 4. Grease a 28 cm x 18 cm x 4 cm / 11" x 7" x 1½" baking tin and line with greaseproof baking paper.

Whisk the eggs and sugar in a mixing bowl. Sift in the flour and baking powder and gently fold into the mixture. Stir in the butter.

Put into the baking tin and shake gently until even. Bake for 30-35 minutes until golden. Turn out onto a wire rack and remove the lining paper. Leave to cool completely.

For the buttercream, melt the chocolate in a heatproof bowl over a pan of simmering water. Remove from the heat and leave to stand for 20 minutes. Whisk the butter in a mixing bowl until fluffy. Whisk in the chocolate and vanilla, until it is smooth. Sift in the icing sugar and whisk until both smooth. Cover and chill for about 40 minutes until thick.

Cut the cake into 3 even pieces. Spread one third of the buttercream on 1 piece and press a quarter of the raspberries into the cream. Place another cake layer on top and repeat the process. Place the remaining cake on top and decorate.

Ingredients

For the cake:
3 eggs
75 g / 2 ½ oz / ⅓ cup caster (superfine) sugar
75 g / 2 ½ oz / ¾ cup plain (all-purpose) flour
½ tsp baking powder
25 g / 1 oz / ⅛ cup butter, melted

For the buttercream:
500 g / 18 oz white chocolate
400 g / 14 oz / 1 ¾ cups butter, unsalted
2 tsp vanilla extract
200 - 250 g / 7 - 9 oz / 2 - 2½ cups icing (confectioners') sugar

To decorate:
250 g / 9 oz / 2 cups raspberries

makes
1

55
mins
preparation and cooking time

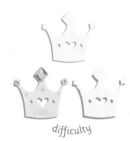

difficulty

Candy Heart Cookies

Method

Heat the oven to 190°C (170° fan) 375F, gas 5. Line a large baking tray with greaseproof baking paper.

Beat the butter and sugar in a mixing bowl until soft and creamy. Gradually beat in the egg and vanilla. Add the flour and mix into a dough. Roll out the dough on a lightly floured surface to a thickness of 1 cm / ½".

Using a heart-shaped cookie cutter, cut cookies out of the dough and place on the baking tray. Bake for 8-10 minutes, until pale golden-brown. Cool on the baking tray for 5 minutes, then place on a wire rack to cool completely.

For the filling, put the jam and lemon juice in a small pan and heat gently until melted. Heat until boiling, and boil the mixture for 2-3 minutes. Set aside to cool and thicken.

For the icing, sift the icing sugar into a bowl and stir in the water. Set a quarter of the icing aside. Dye the remaining icing pink and spread over half of the cookies. Spread the jam on the un-iced cookies and place an iced cookie on top. Drizzle with the reserved white icing and leave to set.

Ingredients

For the cookies:
110 g / 4 oz / ½ cup butter, unsalted
110 g / 4 oz / ½ cup caster (superfine) sugar
1 egg, lightly beaten
1 tsp vanilla extract
275 g / 10 oz / 2 ½ cups plain (all-purpose) flour

For the filling:
135 g apricot jam (jelly)
1 tsp lemon juice

For the icing:
250 g / 9 oz / 2 ½ cups icing (confectioners') sugar
2 - 3 tbsp water
few drops pink food dye

Why not try...
decorating with rose petals for full romantic effect?

difficulty

Scrumptious Crunch Muffins

Method

Mix together the oats and buttermilk and set aside for 1 hour. Heat the oven to 200°C (180° fan) 400F, gas 6. Place paper cases in a 12 hole muffin tin.

Beat the butter and sugar in a mixing bowl until light and fluffy. Beat in the egg until blended. Sift together the flour, cinnamon, baking powder, bicarbonate of soda and the salt. Gently stir into the butter mixture, alternately with the oat mixture. Stir in the raisins.

Spoon into the paper cases and sprinkle the tops lightly with rolled oats. Bake for 20-25 minutes, until risen and golden. Cool in the tin for 5 minutes, then place on a wire rack to cool completely.

Ingredients

110 g / 4 oz / 1 cup rolled oats, plus extra for topping
250 ml / 9 fl. oz / 1 cup buttermilk
110 g / 4 oz / ½ cup butter
80 g / 3 oz / ⅓ cup sugar
1 egg
110 g / 4 oz / 1 cup plain (all-purpose) flour
1 tsp ground cinnamon
1 tsp baking powder
½ tsp bicarbonate of (baking) soda
a pinch of salt
50 g / 1 ¾ oz / ½ cup raisins

Why not try...
serving with yoghurt and sliced banana?

Why not try...

using candy of all different colors, for a rainbow window effect?

Looking-Glass Lollipops

makes
20

25 mins
preparation and cooking time

difficulty

Method

Heat the oven to 180°C (160° fan) 350F, gas 4. Line a large baking tray with greaseproof baking paper.

Beat the butter and sugar in a mixing bowl until soft and creamy. Gradually beat in the egg yolks. Add the flour and salt and mix to form a dough. Wrap in cling film and chill for 30 minutes.

Roll out the dough on a lightly floured surface to a thickness of 1 cm / ½" Using a heart-shaped cookie cutter, cut biscuits out of the dough. Using a smaller heart-shaped cutter, cut out the middle of each heart.

Place on the baking tray. Insert a wooden lollipop stick into the tip of each biscuit, pressing down slightly to let the tip of the stick slightly protrude into the heart. Completely fill the hole in each biscuit with crushed hard candies. Bake for 10-12 minutes, until the biscuit is golden brown and the candy has melted. Cool on the baking tray and remove when cold.

Tie a pink ribbon around each stick.

Ingredients

150 g / 5 oz / ⅔ cup butter
150 g / 5 oz / ⅔ cup sugar
2 egg yolks
250 g / 9 oz / 2 ¼ cups plain
(all-purpose) flour
a pinch of salt
110 g / 4 oz pink hard candies,
lightly crushed

To decorate:
pink ribbons

Why not try...

serving with a gooey
chocolate sauce?

Splendid Spotty Sponge

Method

Put the flour, sugar, salt and yeast into a mixing bowl. Add the melted butter and eggs then gradually beat in the warm milk. Cover the bowl loosely with oiled cling film and leave in a warm place for 1 hour until doubled in size.

Grease a 23 cm / 9" gugelhupf tin. Beat the almonds, candied peel and almond extract into the mixture and pour into the tin. Cover the top of the tin loosely with oiled cling film and leave in a warm place to rise for 45 minutes, until the mixture almost reaches the top of the tin.

Heat the oven to 190°C (170° fan) 375F, gas 5. Remove the cling film and bake for 35-40 minutes. Check after 20 minutes and cover with foil if the cake is becoming too brown. Leave in the tin for 5 minutes, then turn out onto a wire rack to cool.

Decorate with pink marzipan and chocolate beans, as in the photo.

makes

1

1 hour

10 mins

preparation and cooking time

difficulty

Ingredients

400 g / 14 oz / 3 ½ cups strong, white bread flour
75 g / 2 ½ oz / ⅓ cup caster (superfine) sugar
½ tsp salt
2 tsp easy-blend (fast-action) yeast
75 g / 2 ½ oz / ⅓ cup unsalted butter, melted
3 eggs, beaten
150 ml / 5 fl. oz / ⅔ cup warm milk
75 g / 2 ½ oz / 1 cup flaked (slivered) almonds
50 g / 1 ¾ oz / ⅓ cup candied peel, chopped
1 tsp almond extract

To decorate:
500 g / 18 oz pink marzipan
chocolate beans

51

Why not try...

giving your Princess a yellow, blue or green ball gown?

Ball Gown Cake

Method

For the cake, heat the oven to 160°C (140° fan) 325F, gas 3. Grease a 900 ml / 1½ pint pudding basin.

Beat the butter and sugar in a mixing bowl until soft and light. Gradually beat in the eggs and milk. Sift in the flour and cornflour and stir in lightly. Gently stir in the ground almonds. Spoon into the pudding basin and bake for 1-1½ hours until firm. Turn out and cool on a wire rack.

For the decoration, place the Barbie doll head and body into the middle of the top of the cake.

Heat the jam and water in a small pan until the jam has melted. Rub through a sieve and return to the pan. Boil for 1 minute and leave to cool. Roll out the pink sugarpaste into a circle to fit generously over the cake.

Brush the cake with most of the jam glaze and place the pink sugarpaste on the cake. Shape the sugarpaste with your hands, as in the photo. Cut 8-9 white sugarpaste triangles to form the top of the skirt. Dampen the triangles with a little water and attach to the top of the cake.

Attach the chocolate beans and sugar hearts to the skirt with a dab of jam glaze. Decorate further with sugarflowers, white icing and pink sparkling sugar, as in the photo.

Ingredients

For the cake:
225 g / 8 oz / 1 cup butter
225 g / 8 oz / 1 cup caster (superfine) sugar
4 eggs, beaten
2 tbsp milk
225 g / 8 oz / 2 cups self-raising flour
50 g / 1 ¾ oz cornflour (cornstarch)
50 g / 1 ¾ oz / ½ cup ground almonds

For the decoration:
1 Barbie doll, legs removed
175 g / 6 oz jam (jelly)
2 tbsp water
350 g / 12 oz pink sugarpaste
110 g / 4 oz white sugarpaste
chocolate beans
pink and white sugar hearts
pink and white sugar flowers
120 g / 4 oz white piping icing
pink sparkling sugar
paper parasol

Chocolate

Why not try...

eating warmed up with
a glass of cold milk?

Swirly Raspberry Roll

makes
1

45 mins
preparation and cooking time

difficulty

Method

Heat the oven to 220°C (200° fan) 425F, gas 7 and line a baking tray with greaseproof baking paper.

Beat the egg whites and 2 tablespoons of cold water to the stiff peak stage. Add the sugar little by little then fold in the egg yolks. Mix together the flour, cornflour, cocoa powder and baking powder and sieve into the egg white mixture. Fold in gently then spread the mixture onto the baking sheet and bake for around 12 minutes. Invert onto a clean tea towel sprinkled with sugar. Carefully peel off the greaseproof baking paper, roll up and let cool.

Whip the cream and sugar until stiff. Unroll the sponge cake, spread with the cream and scatter with raspberries. Roll up and chill in the refrigerator for at least 3 hours. Serve dusted with icing sugar.

Ingredients

For the sponge:
4 egg whites
125 g / 4 ½ oz / ⅔ cup sugar
4 egg yolks, beaten
80 g / 3 oz / ⅗ cup flour
40 g / 1 ½ oz / ⅓ cup cornflour (cornstarch)
40 g / 1 ½ oz / ¼ cup cocoa powder
1 tsp baking powder
caster (superfine) sugar for rolling

For the filling:
400 ml / 14 fl. oz / 1 ⅔ cups cream
70 g / 2 ½ oz / ⅓ cup sugar
150 g / 5 oz / 1 cup raspberries

To decorate:
icing (confectioners') sugar

Why not try...
cutting into flower or
star shapes instead of hearts?

Iced Brownies

Method

Heat the oven to 180°C (160° fan) 350F, gas 4. Line the base and sides of a 30 cm x 22 cm / 12" x 9" roasting tin with greaseproof baking paper.

Melt the chocolate in a heatproof bowl over a pan of simmering water. Remove from the heat. Beat the butter and sugar in a mixing bowl until light and fluffy. Whisk in the whole eggs and yolk, and stir in the chocolate and coffee. Sift in the flour and baking powder and gently stir into the mixture with the salt. Spoon into the tin and bake for 25-30 minutes. Leave to cool in the tin.

For the icing, put the strawberries into a pan with the water and sugar. Simmer on a high heat for about 3 minutes until the strawberries are soft. Remove from the heat and mash. Stir the marshmallows into the hot pulp until they dissolve, and leave to cool.

Whisk the cream until it holds its shape, but is not stiff. Fold the cream into the cooled strawberry mixture, and chill for 1-2 hours until thick.

Cut out heart shapes from the cake, using a cookie cutter. Place a spoonful of the strawberry mousse on top of the hearts and spread fairly thickly. Chill until the mousse has set. Decorate with sugar hearts and chocolate flakes.

Ingredients

For the brownies:
200 g / 7 oz plain (dark) chocolate
125 g / 4 ½ oz / ½ cup butter, unsalted
225 g / 8 oz / 1 cup caster (superfine) sugar
2 eggs
1 egg yolk
30 ml freshly made instant coffee
150 g / 5 oz / 1 ¼ cups plain (all-purpose) flour
1 tsp baking powder
a pinch of salt

For the icing:
250 g / 9 oz / 1 ¼ cups strawberries, sliced
100 ml / 3 ½ fl. oz water
2 tbsp sugar
140 g / 5 oz / 2 cups mini marshmallows
200 ml / 7 fl. oz / ⅞ cup cream

To decorate:
pink sugar hearts
chocolate flakes

makes
8

50 mins

preparation and cooking time

difficulty

makes

1

15
mins

preparation and cooking time

difficulty

Glittery Crunch Cake

Method

Line a loaf tin with cling film. Melt the butter and syrup in a small pan. Stir and remove from the heat.

Melt the chocolate in a heatproof bowl over a pan of simmering (not boiling) water. Remove from the heat and mix with the buttery syrup.

Stir in the biscuits and raisins and put the mix into the tin. Smooth the top and scatter with the sugar crystals. Chill for at least 4 hours until set.

Cut into slices to serve.

Ingredients

250 g / 9 oz / 1 ⅛ cups butter, unsalted
175 ml / 6 fl. oz / ¾ cup golden syrup
400 g / 14 oz plain (dark) chocolate
200 g / 7 oz digestive biscuits (sweetmeal cookies), broken into small pieces
100 g / 3 ½ oz / ¾ cup raisins
pink sugar crystals

Why not try...

adding walnuts or pistachios for extra crunch?

makes

15

45
mins

preparation and cooking time

difficulty

Splendidly Silky Caramel Slices

Method

Heat the oven to 180°C (160° fan) 350F, gas 4. Lightly grease a 33 cm x 23 cm / 13" x 9" Swiss roll (jelly roll) tin.

For the shortbread, mix the flour and sugar in a mixing bowl. Rub in the butter until the mixture resembles breadcrumbs. Knead the mixture together to form a dough, then press into the base of the tin. Prick lightly with a fork and bake for about 20 minutes, until firm to the touch and very lightly browned. Cool in the tin.

For the caramel, put the butter, sugar and condensed milk into a pan and heat gently until the sugar has dissolved. Heat until boiling, stirring constantly, then reduce the heat and simmer very gently, stilll stirring continuously, for 5-8 minutes until thick. Pour over the shortbread and leave to cool. Chill until firm.

For the topping, melt the plain chocolate in a heatproof bowl over a pan of simmering (not boiling) water. Remove from the heat and leave to cool slightly. Pour over the cold caramel and leave to set.

Melt the white chocolate as before and drizzle fine lines over the top of the plain chocolate. Leave to set, then cut into squares.

Ingredients

For the shortbread base:
250 g / 9 oz / 2 ¼ cups plain (all-purpose) flour
75 g / 2 ½ oz / ⅓ cup caster (superfine) sugar
175 g / 6 oz / ¾ cup butter

For the caramel:
100 g / 3 ½ oz / ½ cup butter
100 g / 3 ½ oz / ½ cup light brown sugar
2 x 397g cans condensed milk

For the topping:
200 g / 7 oz plain (dark) chocolate
110 g / 4 oz white chocolate

Why not try...
swirling different white chocolate patterns into the dark chocolate tops?

Why not try...
drizzling with melted white chocolate instead?

Chocolate Waterfall Cake

makes **1**

1 hour **40 mins**

preparation and cooking time

difficulty

Method

For the cake, heat the oven to 160°C (140° fan) 325F, gas 3. Grease a 2 litre / 3 pint pudding bowl.

Beat the butter and sugar in a mixing bowl until soft and creamy. Add the eggs, one at a time, beating well between each addition.

Sift in the flour and cocoa and stir well until combined. Pour the mixture into the bowl and bake for about 1¼ hours until firm and risen. Cool in the bowl for 10 minutes, then turn out onto a wire rack to cool completely.

For the topping, put the butter, milk and cocoa into a pan and heat gently, stirring, until the butter has melted. Remove and allow to cool slightly.

Gradually sift in the icing sugar, beating until smooth. Pour over the cake, allowing it to run down the sides. Decorate with pink candy before the topping sets.

Ingredients

For the cake:
250 g / 9 oz / 1 ⅛ cups butter
250 g / 9 oz / 1 ⅛ cups caster (superfine) sugar
4 eggs
325 g / 11 oz / 2 ¾ cups self-raising flour
50 g / 1 ¾ oz / ½ cup cocoa powder

For the topping:
110 g / 4 oz / ½ cup butter
60 ml / 2 fl. oz milk
60 ml / 2 fl. oz cocoa powder
400 - 450 g / 14 - 16 oz / 4 cups icing (confectioners') sugar

To decorate:
pink candy

Why not try...

decorating with flaked almonds
or chopped hazelnuts?

Sparkling Sprinkle Bites

Method

Heat the oven to 180°C (160° fan) 350F, gas 4.
Line a large baking tray with greaseproof baking paper.

Beat the butter and sugar in a mixing bowl until light and fluffy.

Add the remaining ingredients and mix well. Roll spoonfuls of the mixture into small balls with your hands. Place the balls well apart on the baking tray and flatten slightly.

Bake for 10 minutes. Cool on the baking tray for a few minutes, then place on a wire rack to cool completely.

For the topping, beat the butter in a large bowl until soft. Sift in half the icing sugar and beat until smooth.

Sift in the remaining icing sugar and cocoa with 1 tablespoon of milk and beat until creamy. Beat in more milk if necessary to loosen the mixture.

Spread the topping on the biscuits and decorate with sugar hearts and sprinkles.

Ingredients

For the biscuits:
110 g / 4 oz / ½ cup butter, unsalted
110 g / 4 oz / ½ cup light brown sugar
1 egg, beaten
75 g / 2 ½ oz / ¾ cup plain (all-purpose) flour
25 g / 1 oz / ¼ cup cocoa powder
½ tsp bicarbonate of (baking) soda
110 g / 4 oz / 1 cup rolled oats

For the topping:
110 g / 4 oz / ½ cup butter, unsalted
170 g / 6 oz / 1 ¾ cups icing (confectioners') sugar
55 g / 2 oz / ½ cup cocoa powder
1 - 2 tbsp milk

To decorate:
pink sugar hearts
sugar sprinkles

Royal Rocky Road

Method

Line a 23 cm / 9″ square tin with cling film.

Melt the plain and milk chocolate in a pan with the syrup and butter over a low heat, stirring constantly. Remove from the heat and allow to cool slightly.

Stir in the shortbread pieces, marshmallows and nuts and spoon into the tin. Chill for at least 2 hours until set. Cut into small squares.

Ingredients

300 g / 11 oz plain (dark) chocolate
100 g / 3 ½ oz milk chocolate
60 ml / 2 fl. oz maple syrup
150 g / 5 oz / ⅔ cup butter
175 g / 6 oz shortbread cookies, broken into small pieces
150 g / 5 oz / 3 cups mini marshmallows, pink and white
150 g / 5 oz / 1 cup pecan nuts, roughly chopped

Why not try...

using soft candy instead of nuts and cookies, for a chewier rocky road?

makes

6

45 mins

preparation and cooking time

difficulty

Chocolate Castle Cakes

Method

Heat the oven to 180°C (160° fan) 350F, gas 4. Grease 6 mini Bundt cake tins or moulds.

Mix together the flour, cocoa, sugar, bicarbonate of soda and salt. Whisk together the egg yolks, water, and oil in a mixing bowl until well blended. Whisk in a third of the flour mixture and stir until just combined. Add another third of the flour mixture and whisk again. Add the remaining mixture and whisk until just combined.

Whisk the egg whites until softly peaking. Add the cream of tartar and whisk until stiff. Gradually fold the egg whites into the egg mixture until blended.

Spoon into the tins and bake for 25-30 minutes, until a wooden cocktail stick inserted into the middle comes out clean. Place the tins on a wire rack to cool for 10 minutes. Remove the cakes from the tins and cool completely.

For the sauce, put the cream in a pan and boil. Remove from the heat and add the chocolate. Leave to stand for a few minutes until melted. Stir in the vanilla.

Place the cakes on a serving plate and spoon a little chocolate sauce over each cake. Decorate with raspberries and coconut.

Ingredients

For the cakes:
75 g / 2 ½ oz / ¾ cup plain (all-purpose) flour
25 g / 1 oz / ¼ cup cocoa powder
110 g / 4 oz / ½ cup sugar
1 tsp bicarbonate of (baking) soda
¼ tsp salt
2 egg yolks
75 ml / 2 ½ fl. oz water
2 tbsp sunflower oil
4 egg whites
¼ tsp cream of tartar

For the sauce:
125 g / 4 ½ oz plain (dark) chocolate
125 ml / 4 ½ fl. oz / ½ cup cream
few drops vanilla extract

To decorate:
raspberries
60 ml / 2 fl. oz grated coconut

Why not try...
decorating with strawberries
or blueberries instead?

Why not try...

filling with ice-cream for
a summery treat?

Sweetheart Cake

55 mins

preparation and cooking time

difficulty

Method

Heat the oven to 180°C (160° fan) 350F, gas 4. Grease and line the base of a 20 cm / 8" heart-shaped (or round) cake tin.

Beat the butter and sugar in a mixing bowl until light and creamy. Gradually beat in the eggs and milk, alternately with a spoonful of flour. Sift in the remaining flour and cocoa and gently stir until well mixed.

Spoon into the tin and level the top. Bake for 35-40 minutes. Leave to cool in the tin for 5 minutes, then place on a wire rack to cool completely.

For the filling, whisk the cream until thick. Gently stir in the raspberries. Slice the cake in half through the middle and spread the cream mixture over the bottom half. Place the other cake half on top and press down lightly.

For the topping, melt the chocolate and butter in a heatproof bowl over a pan of simmering (not boiling) water. Remove from the heat and leave to cool. Spread over the top of the cake and leave to set. Decorate with berries and petals.

Ingredients

For the cake:
175 g / 6 oz / ¾ cup butter, unsalted
175 g / 6 oz / ¾ cup caster (superfine) sugar
3 large eggs, beaten
2 tbsp milk
175 g / 6 oz / 1 ½ cups self-raising flour
25 g / 1 oz / ¼ cup cocoa powder

For the filling:
200 ml / 7 fl. oz / ⅞ cup cream
150 g / 5 oz / 1 ¼ cups raspberries

For the topping:
100 g / 3 ½ oz plain (dark) chocolate
25 g / 1 oz / ⅛ cup butter, unsalted

To decorate:
raspberries
rose petals

Cupcakes

Why not try...
decorating with edible glitter? Fabulous!

Fairy-dust Fancies

Method

For the fairy cakes, heat the oven to 160°C (140° fan) 325F, gas 3. Place paper cases in a 12 hole bun tin.

Put all the cake ingredients into a mixing bowl and whisk until well combined. Alternatively, beat well with a wooden spoon. Spoon the mixture into the paper cases and bake for 25-30 minutes until golden and springy to the touch. Remove from the tin and place on a wire rack to cool completely.

For the chocolate buttercream, beat the butter in a large bowl until soft. Sift in the icing sugar and beat until smooth. Sift in the cocoa and beat well. Stir in the milk until creamy. Add more milk if necessary to loosen the mixture.

For the vanilla buttercream, beat the butter until soft. Sift in the icing sugar and beat until smooth. Stir in the vanilla. Spread the buttercream on top of the cakes. Decorate with sugar flowers, sprinkles and baubles.

Ingredients

For the fairy cakes:
2 eggs
110 g / 4 oz / 1 cup self-raising flour
½ tsp baking powder
110 g / 4 oz / ½ cup butter, softened
110 g / 4 oz / ½ cup sugar
1 tsp vanilla extract

For the chocolate buttercream:
50 g / 1 ¾ oz / ¼ cup butter, unsalted
75 g / 2 ½ oz / ⅔ cup icing (confectioners') sugar
25 g / 1 oz / ¼ cup cocoa powder
½ - 1 tbsp milk

For the vanilla buttercream:
75 g / 2 ½ oz / ⅓ cup butter, unsalted
125 g / 4 ½ oz / 1 ¼ cups icing (confectioners') sugar
few drops vanilla extract

To decorate:
sugar flowers
sugar sprinkles
silver baubles

Gooey Red Gem Muffins

Method

Heat the oven to 190°C (170° fan) 375F, gas 5. Line a 12 hole muffin tin with muffin cups or paper cases.

Put the cream, sugar, eggs and vanilla into a mixing bowl and whisk with an electric whisk for about 5 minutes until smooth. Stir in the flour and baking powder until just combined. Gently stir in the strawberries and redcurrants.

Spoon into the muffin cups and bake for 25-30 minutes until golden and risen. Cool in the tins for 5 minutes, then place on a wire rack to cool completely.

Sift over a little icing sugar just before serving.

Ingredients

280 ml / 10 fl. oz / 1 ¼ cups cream
200 g / 7 oz / 1 cup caster (superfine) sugar
2 eggs
1 tsp vanilla extract
400 g / 14 oz / 3 ½ cups plain (all-purpose) flour
3 tsp baking powder
100 g / 3 ½ oz / ½ cup strawberries, sliced
100 g / 3 ½ oz / ½ cup redcurrants

To decorate:
icing (confectioners') sugar

makes
12

40 mins

preparation and cooking time

difficulty

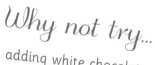

Why not try...

adding white chocolate chips to the mix for an extra treat?

Why not try...

decorating with other gummy candies to make different animals?

Beautiful Butterfly Cupcakes

makes
12

50 mins

preparation and cooking time

Method

For the cupcakes, heat the oven to 170°C (150° fan) 325F, gas 3. Place paper cases in a 12 hole bun tin.

Put all of the cupcake ingredients into a mixing bowl and whisk with an electric whisk until well combined. Alternatively, beat well with a wooden spoon. Spoon the mixture into the paper cases and bake for 20-25 minutes until golden and springy to the touch. Remove from the tin and place on a wire rack to cool.

For the decoration, beat the butter until soft and creamy. Sift in the icing sugar and beat well. Stir in the vanilla. Put half the buttercream into a small bowl and stir in a few drops of green food dye.

Spread the buttercream over the top of the cooled cupcakes, 6 green and 6 plain. Place 2 fruit jelly slices on each cake to form 'wings'.

Cut the remaining fruit jelly slices into 3 and roll between your hands to form the 'body' shapes. Use 2 contrasting dyes to form the body and place between the fruit jelly slices. Mark the 'body' evenly with a knife to form rings, as in the photo. Add 2 fruit candies to each cake for the caterpillar 'feelers'.

difficulty

Ingredients

For the cupcakes:

2 eggs
110 g / 4 oz / 1 cup self-raising flour
½ tsp baking powder
110 g / 4 oz / ½ cup butter, softened
110 g / 4 oz / ½ cup sugar

To decorate:
110 g / 4 oz / ½ cup butter
225 g / 8 oz / 2 ¼ cups icing (confectioners') sugar
½ tsp vanilla extract
green food dye
32 assorted mini fruit jelly slices
24 assorted chewy fruit candies

makes
12

45 mins

preparation and cooking time

difficulty

Pink Palace Muffins

Method

Heat the oven to 180°C (160° fan) 350F, gas 4. Place paper cases in a 12 hole muffin tin.

Mix together the flour, ground almonds, baking powder and bicarbonate of soda in a bowl. Whisk the eggs lightly in a mixing bowl. Stir in the sugar, oil, soured cream and rosewater, mixing well.

Stir in the dry ingredients and stir until just combined. The mixture will be lumpy. Spoon into the paper cases and bake for about 25 minutes until golden and risen. Cool in the tins for 5 minutes, then place on a wire rack to cool completely. (Slice the peaked top off each muffin, so that the muffins are flat.)

Roll out the sugarpaste on a surface lightly dusted with icing sugar. Cut out 12 circles, the same size as the tops of the muffins. Dampen one side of the sugarpaste circles and place on top of the muffins, smoothing out.

Knead together the scraps of sugarpaste and roll out as before. Cut out flowers with a sugarpaste flower cutter and attach to the top of each muffin with a little water. Place a white candy in the middle of each flower.

Ingredients

250 g / 9 oz / 2 ¼ cups plain (all-purpose) flour
50 g / 1 ¾ oz / ½ cup ground almonds
2 tsp baking powder
½ tsp bicarbonate of (baking) soda
2 eggs
110 g / 4 oz / ½ cup sugar
80 ml / 3 fl. oz / ⅓ cup sunflower oil
125 ml / 4 ½ fl. oz / ½ cup soured cream
1 tbsp rosewater

To decorate:
icing (confectioners') sugar
250 g / 9 oz pink sugarpaste
12 white candies

Why not try...

using blue sugarpaste
to make muffins
fit for a Prince?

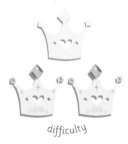

difficulty

Dainty Daisy Cakes

Method

For the cupcakes, heat the oven to 180°C (160° fan) 350F, gas 4. Place paper cases in a 12 hole bun tin.

Sift the flour, sugar and baking powder into a mixing bowl. Whisk together the egg, milk, oil and vanilla. Stir into the dry ingredients until combined.

Spoon into the paper cases and bake for about 20 minutes until golden and risen. Cool in the tin for 5 minutes then place on a wire rack to cool completely.

For the decoration, divide the white sugarpaste in half. Then divide one half again into as many different colored bases as you would like to make. Knead a few drops of food dye into the sugarpaste to make it your chosen color. Roll out each colored block of sugarpaste and cut out circles slightly smaller than the tops of the cakes.

Brush the tops of the cakes with a little jam and attach the sugarpaste circles.

Roll out the remaining white sugarpaste thinly. Cut out 8 'petals' for each cake. Mark a line down the middle of each 'petal' with a sharp knife. Attach to the cakes as shown in the picture, using a dab of jam.

For the yellow centre circles, reserve some white sugarpaste and dye it yellow. Roll small pieces of the yellow sugarpaste into 12 small circles for the middle of the 'flower' and attach in the middle of the 'petals' with a little jam. Decorate with dots of white icing.

Ingredients

For the cupcakes:
225 g / 8 oz / 2 cups plain (all-purpose) flour
110 g / 4 oz / ½ cup caster (superfine) sugar
2 tsp baking powder
1 egg, beaten
150 ml / 5 fl. oz / ⅔ cup milk
50 ml / 1 ¾ fl. oz / 10 tsp sunflower oil
1 tsp vanilla extract

For the decoration:
450 g / 16 oz white sugarpaste
colored food dyes
1-2 tbsp jam (jelly), warmed

Why not try...

♡ making exotic sugarpaste flowers in blues, oranges and purples?

Magnificent Muffins

difficulty

Method

Heat the oven to 200°C (180° fan) 400F, gas 6. Place paper cases in a 12 hole muffin tin.

Beat the egg in a mixing bowl and then beat in the sugar, milk and vanilla. Gradually beat in the butter until combined. Sift in the flour, baking powder and salt and stir quickly until just combined. The mixture will be lumpy.

Pour the mixture into the paper cases and bake for about 20 minutes, until risen and golden. Cool in the tin for 5 minutes, then place on a wire rack to cool completely.

For the icing, sift the icing sugar into a bowl and gradually stir in the lemon juice and water until smooth. Add a few drops of green food dye and stir. Spoon the icing onto the muffins, and leave to set.

For the decoration, roll out the different sugarpastes separately, and cut out flower shapes.

Dampen the base of each flower with a little water and attach to the icing. Place a coloured candy in the middle of each flower.

Ingredients

For the muffins:
1 large egg
110 g / 4 oz / ½ cup sugar
230 ml / 8 fl.oz / 1 cup milk
1 tsp vanilla extract
110 g / 4 oz / ½ cup butter, melted and cooled
225 g / 8 oz / 2 cups plain (all-purpose) flour
1 tbsp baking powder
½ tsp salt

For the icing:
200 g / 7 oz / 2 cups icing (confectioners') sugar
1 tsp lemon juice
2-3 tbsp water
green food dye

For the decoration:
250 g / 9 oz white sugarpaste
250 g / 9 oz pink sugarpaste
250 g / 9 oz yellow sugarpaste
12 small hard candies, white, pink and yellow

Why not try...

tying a tag to the ribbon and giving these cupcakes as presents?

Belle of the Ball Cupcakes

difficulty

Method

For the cupcakes, heat the oven to 160°C (140° fan) 325F, gas 3. Place paper cases in a 12 hole bun tin.

For the cupcakes, put all the ingredients into a mixing bowl and whisk with an electric whisk until well combined. Alternatively, beat well with a wooden spoon.

Spoon the mixture into the paper cases and bake for 20-25 minutes until golden and springy to the touch. Remove from the tin and place on a wire rack to cool completely.

For the icing, sift the icing sugar into a bowl and gradually stir in the water and vanilla until smooth and thick enough to coat the back of a spoon. Spoon the icing onto the cakes and spread evenly. Leave to set.

To decorate, tie a ribbon around each cake.

Ingredients

For the cupcakes:
2 eggs
110 g / 4 oz / 1 cup self-raising flour
½ tsp baking powder
110 g / 4 oz / ½ cup butter, softened
110 g / 4 oz / ½ cup sugar
1 tsp vanilla extract

For the icing:
200 g / 7 oz / 2 cups icing (confectioners') sugar
2-3 tbsp water
1 tsp vanilla extract

For the decoration:
12 pink ribbons

Why not try...

using black and white sugarpaste squares to make chessboard cupcakes?

Pink Diamond Delights

Method

For the cupcakes, heat the oven to 180°C (160° fan) 350F, gas 4. Place paper cases in a 10 hole bun tin.

Whisk the eggs and sugar until light, then beat in the cream and vanilla. Sift over the flour and baking powder and gently stir in. Stir in the butter, until well blended.

Spoon into the paper cases and bake for 12-15 minutes until golden and springy to the touch. Leave to cool in the tins for 5 minutes, then turn out onto a wire rack to cool completely.

For the decoration, lightly roll out the white sugarpaste on a surface lightly dusted with icing sugar. Cut into small squares. Repeat with the pink sugarpaste, cutting out the same number of squares.

Gently warm the jam and brush over the cupcakes. Arrange the sugarpaste squares on top of each cake, alternating pink and white, to form a checkerboard pattern, as in the photo. Place a sugar flower on each cake.

makes
10

45 mins

preparation and cooking time

difficulty

Ingredients

For the cupcakes:
2 eggs
110 g / 4 oz / ½ cup caster (superfine) sugar
55 ml / 2 fl. oz / 11 tsp cream
1 tsp vanilla extract
110 g / 4 oz / 1 cup self-raising flour
½ tsp baking powder
55 g / 2 oz / ¼ cup butter, melted and cooled

For the decoration:
icing (confectioners') sugar
500 g / 18 oz white sugarpaste
500 g / 18 oz pink sugarpaste
2 tbsp jam (jelly)
10 sugar flowers

makes
10

30 mins

preparation and cooking time

difficulty

Snowy-Peak Sparkle Cakes

Method

Heat the oven to 180°C (160° fan) 350F, gas 4. Place paper cases in a 10 hole muffin tin.

Sift the flour and baking powder into a mixing bowl. Whisk together the sugar, egg yolks, oil, milk, lemon juice and zest until smooth. Stir into the flour. Whisk the egg whites until stiff and gently fold into the mixture until just combined. Stir in the redcurrants. Spoon into the paper cases.

For the meringue, reserve about 2 teaspoons of egg white. Whisk the remaining egg whites until they stand in soft peaks. Gradually whisk in the sugar until the mixture is stiff. Spoon on top of the muffins and bake for 15-20 minutes until the meringue is crisp and browned and the muffins are cooked. Place on a wire rack to cool completely.

To decorate, Lightly beat the reserved egg white. Roll the redcurrants in the egg white, then in the sugar. Leave to dry. Place a few redcurrants on top of each muffin and place some frosted redcurrants on the serving plate.

Ingredients

For the muffins:
175 g / 6 oz / 1 ½ cups plain (all-purpose) flour
2 tsp baking powder
140 g / 5 oz / ⅔ cup caster (superfine) sugar
2 eggs, separated
120 ml / 4 fl. oz sunflower oil
90 ml / 3 fl. oz milk
½ lemon, juiced and finely grated zest
170 g / 6 oz / 1 ½ cups redcurrants

For the meringue:
2 egg whites
100 g / 3 ½ oz / ½ cup caster (superfine) sugar

To decorate:
redcurrants
sugar

Why not try...
serving with fruit teas
and pouring cream?

difficulty

Romantic Rose Cupcakes

Method

For the cupcakes, heat the oven to 180°C (160° fan) 350F, gas 4. Place paper cups or cases in a 10 hole bun tin.

Beat the marzipan, butter and sugar in a mixing bowl to a smooth paste. Whisk in the eggs gradually, whisking constantly until the mixture is smooth. Gently fold in the rosewater, almonds, flour and baking powder until well blended.

Spoon the mixture into the paper cases and bake for 20-25 minutes until risen and springy to the touch. Cool in the tin for 5 minutes, then place on a wire rack to cool completely.

For the roses, roll out the sugarpaste thinly on a surface lightly dusted with icing sugar. Cut out 60 circles.

Roll 1 circle into a cone shape. Roll another circle around the cone, gently pushing the two together so they stick. Pinch out the top of the circles so they curl over slightly, to create a petal shape. Continue to wrap the sugarpaste circles around the previous ones, pressing and pinching as before. Tweak out all the petals as you work, to look like a rose. Use 6 sugarpaste circles for each rose.

Place the roses on top of the cakes.

Ingredients

For the cupcakes:
225 g / 8 oz marzipan, finely chopped
75 g / 2 ½ oz / ⅓ cup butter, unsalted
100 g / 3 ½ oz / ½ cup caster (superfine) sugar
3 eggs, beaten
1 tbsp milk
100 g / 3 ½ oz / ¾ cup ground almonds
150 g / 5 oz / 1 ¼ cups plain (all-purpose) flour
2 tsp baking powder
1 tsp rosewater

For the roses:
icing (confectioners') sugar
500 g / 18 oz pink sugarpaste

Why not try...

serving with chilled
lemonade, for the perfect
summer treat?

Index

Almonds, 20-21, 30-31, 36-37, 38-39, 40-41, 50-51, 52-53, 82-83, 94-95
Apricot, 10-11, 36-37

Banana, 10-11
Basil, 16-17

Candy, 48-49, 52-53, 64-65, 80-81, 82-83, 86-87
Carrot, 14-15, 18-19
Cheese, Cheddar, 12-13, 16-17, 22-23, 26-27, 28-29
Cheese, cream, 16-17
Cheese, Parmesan, 8-9, 26-27
Chicken, 8-9, 18-19,
Chocolate, 38-39, 42-43, 58-59, 60-61, 62-63, 68-69, 70-71, 72-73
Cocoa powder, 56-57, 64-65, 66-67, 70-71, 72-73, 76-77
Coconut, 34-35, 38-39, 70-71
Coffee, 58-59
Courgette, 30-31
Cranberries, 14-15, 24-25
Cream, 26-27, 56-57, 58-59, 70-71, 72-73, 78-79, 90-91

Ginger, 20-21

Ham, 26-27, 28-29
Honey, 36-37

Jam, 40-41, 43-44, 52-53, 84-85, 90-91

Lemon, 10-11, 30-31, 44-45, 86-87, 92-93

Marshmallows, 58-59, 68-69
Marzipan, 50-51, 94-95
Oats, 36-37, 46-47, 66-67
Onion, 12-13, 18-19, 22-23, 26-27
Orange, 14-15, 24-25

Pasta, 26-27
Pastry, 16-17, 22-23
Peanut butter, 36-37
Pecan nuts, 68-69
Peppers, 28-29

Raisins, 10-11, 36-37, 46-47, 60-61
Raspberries, 34-35, 42-43, 56-57, 70-71, 72-73
Redcurrants, 78-79, 92-93
Rhubarb, 20-21
Rosewater, 82-83, 94-95

Sesame seeds, 36-37
Soured cream, 82-83
Strawberries, 58-59, 78-79
Sugarpaste, 52-53, 82-83, 84-85, 86-87, 90-91, 94-95
Sweetcorn, 18-19

Tomato, 13-14, 16-17
Tortilla chips, 12-13